THIS BOOK BELONGS TO

....

For Zoë, thank you for putting up with me over lockdown.

Special thanks to Zoë, Jim, Michelle, Kit, Alex, Mum, Jennie Crawley,
Dr Chan Aye, Phonge, the oozies I met and the Flying Eye Team.

BANDOOLA

THE GREAT ELEPHANT RESCUE

William Grill

FLYING EYE BOOKS

LONDON | LOS ANGELES

MYANMAR

CONTENTS

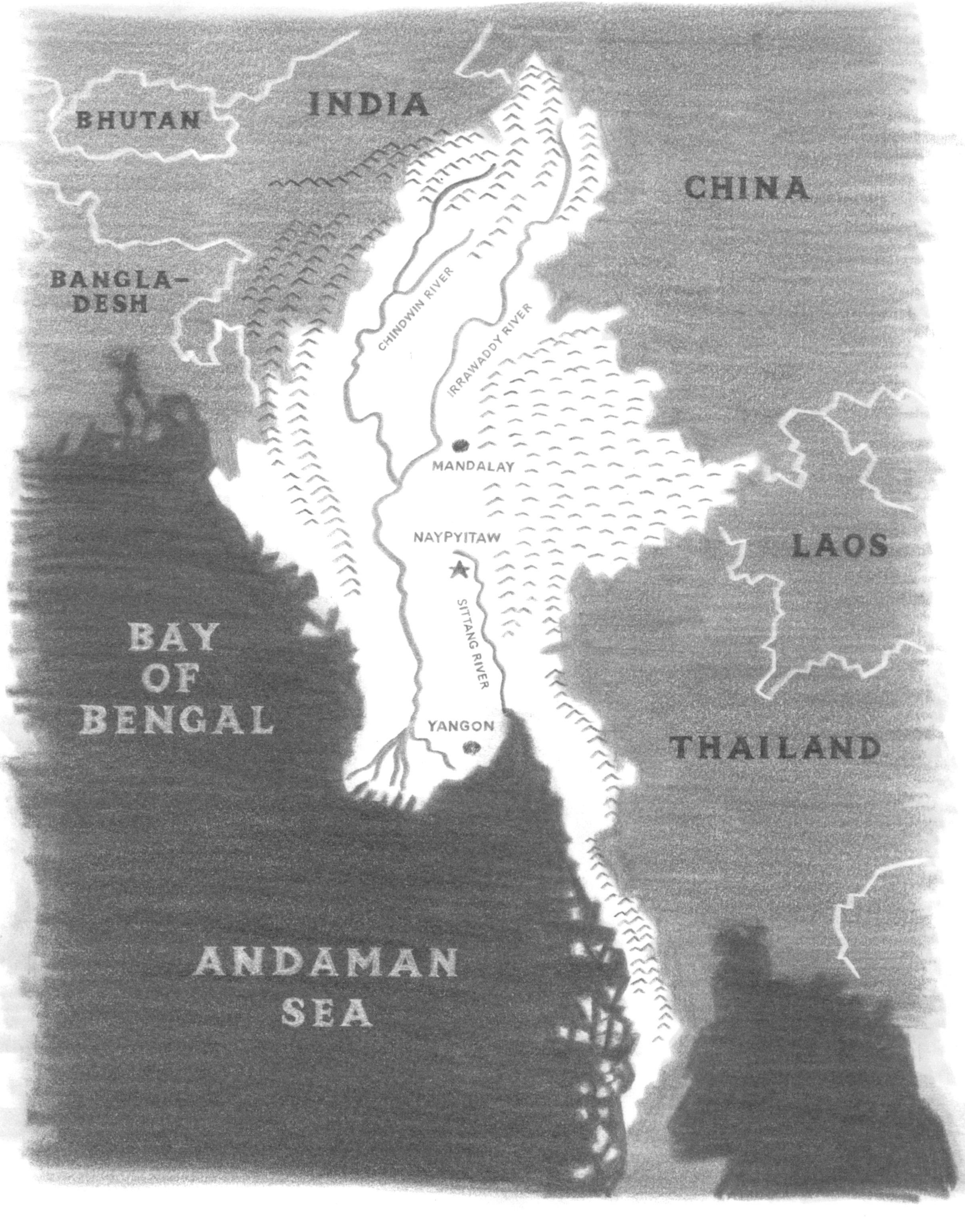
INDIA
BHUTAN
CHINA
BANGLA-
DESH
CHINDWIN RIVER
IRRAWADDY RIVER
MANDALAY
NAYPYITAW
SITTANG RIVER
LAOS
BAY
OF
BENGAL
YANGON
THAILAND
ANDAMAN
SEA

FOREWORD

Myanmar is a country in South-east Asia, nestled between India, Bangladesh, China, Laos and Thailand. The country is famous for its vast forests, which provide important habitats for wildlife. Sadly, today many of these forests are being cut down by humans to make way for farms or to use the wood to make buildings, paper or furniture. This is called deforestation.

From 1824 to 1948, Myanmar was a colony of the British Empire and the country was renamed Burma. On 4th January 1948, Myanmar celebrated its independence. Throughout this book, we will refer to it as Myanmar.

Before the British arrived, Myanmar had grown all its own food, mostly on small farms. Under British rule, it became a land of trade and export, selling goods and resources to other countries all over the world. Although the country saw growth and development, most of the wealth was enjoyed by the British Empire and disrupted the way of life for the people of Myanmar. The negative impacts of the British occupation of Myanmar are still felt in the country today.

This story takes place when the British Empire profited by exploiting Myanmar's land, which was rich in natural resources such as oil, gas, jade, rubies, tin and, most importantly for our story, timber.

Timber was Myanmar's most valuable resource, especially the exotic hardwood teak. This rich nut- brown wood was highly valued because of its strength, water resistance and beauty. It was perfect for building ships and other hard-wearing objects. Since much of the world's teak originated from Myanmar's forests, it is now illegal to sell it to other countries.

INTRODUCTION

From 1990-2010, Myanmar lost 20% of its forest cover through deforestation. Around half of Myanmar still remains covered with forests. It has a varied climate, split into cool, hot and rainy seasons. The country contains a wide variety of habitats, called biomes, which are bursting with animal and plant life.

Tidal forest 4%

Mixed deciduous forest 39%

Dry forest 10%

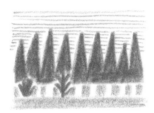

Hill and temperate forest 26%

Tropical evergreen forest 16%

Deciduous dipterocarp forest 5%

These biomes, especially the forests in the north, are important shelters for species such as:

Asian elephant

Indochinese leopard

Eld's deer

Saltwater crocodile

Burmese roofed turtle

Sun bear

White-rumped vulture

Burmese python

Water buffalo

Indochinese tiger

Myanmar snub-nosed monkey

Gaur

Red panda

Malayan tapir

Sunda pangolin

Yellow-throated marten

Elephants are of great cultural and historic importance in Myanmar, where 90% of the population are Buddhist. Buddhists believe that elephants are strong, wise and patient, just like Buddha, the spiritual leader who founded the religion.

Elephants are also economically vital to Myanmar, as they are trained to carry out difficult work, such as harvesting and transporting wood.

Today, many people believe that animals should not be forced to work for humans. Timber elephants are illegal in most countries except in Myanmar where their numbers are dwindling. However, at the time our story is set, it was an important way of life for many in Myanmar.

This is a true story about one of those elephants. A great hero who would change the lives of those around him and leave a legacy that encourages us to protect and celebrate these remarkable animals. This is the incredible story of Bandoola and the Great Elephant Rescue.

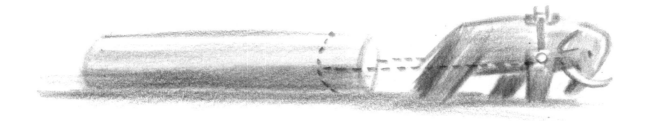

BANDOOLA & ELEPHANT BILL

This story begins in 1897 when an extraordinary elephant was born in the jungles of Myanmar. In that very same year, over 8,000 kilometres away in England, a boy named James Howard Williams was also born. At that time, nobody would predict the incredible bond, nor the amazing adventures, that they would have together in the years to come.

Bandoola was a male Indian elephant, known as a tusker. He had a sprinkle of pale pink freckles across his cheeks and trunk. Bandoola would grow to be one of the strongest and most intelligent elephants in the jungle. His exploits would earn him fame long after he was gone, and in his own lifetime he was respected by all that knew him.

From an early age Williams loved animals. He always tried to see life through their eyes. As a boy, his first animal friend was a donkey named Prince, who he could always find on the Cornish moorlands, near his home. When World War I broke out in 1914, Williams enlisted in the British Army. He served in North Africa, the Middle East, India and Afghanistan. During his war years he found a faithful companion in his beloved camel, Frying Pan.

Like many of the young men lucky enough to survive World War I, Williams was troubled by his experiences and never spoke of them again. He had, however, enjoyed travelling and so, after the war was over, he applied for a job with the Bombay Burma Trading Corporation (BBTC). The company chopped down and transported wood from towering teak trees in Myanmar, aided by thousands of elephants. Williams couldn't wait to meet these gentle giants. Little did he know that one day he would become a household name in Britain, known as "Elephant Bill".

Jungles of central Myanmar, along the Chindwin River, 1920

ELEPHANT CAMP

Despite hearing tales of ghost tigers, deadly diseases and creeping madness brought on by the lonely jungle, Williams was excited to start his new job in the Myanmar rainforest in 1920. He was posted on the upper banks of the Chindwin River, where his role was to oversee the harvesting and transporting of precious teak from the jungle. He was responsible for a work division with 70 elephants. They were split into seven teams along with their riders, known as oozies, who lived with their families in the elephant camps.

Most new arrivals who took up this role quit after a few months. However, Williams flourished. He had a great respect for the oozies, who taught him how to care for the elephants. He watched and listened as they worked, trying to learn everything he could from them, and was amazed by their skills and knowledge. Williams came to know over one thousand elephants by name.

ELEPHANT WATCH

By day Williams worked to harvest teak wood, but at night he had the opportunity to absorb everything there was to learn about elephants. In the pale moonlight, he observed them as they silently wandered and foraged. For a brief moment, they were free, like their wild cousins. Williams hadn't expected them to be so magnetic and peaceful to watch; there was more to these animals than he'd ever imagined.

AN AMAZING ANIMAL

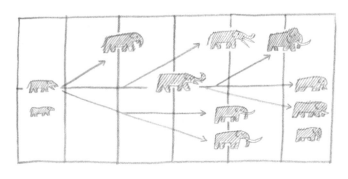

Elephants belong to an ancient family of animals with long trunks, called Proboscidea. All have become extinct except three species: African savanna, African forest and Asian elephants. Asian elephants differ from African elephants in a few ways.

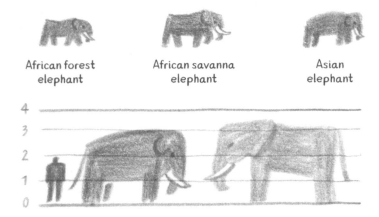

Asian elephants are generally shorter and lighter, whereas African elephants are heavier and taller.

African elephants weigh up to 7,000 kilograms, which is around four times as heavy as a car! Asian elephants weigh up to 5,000 kilograms.

Their body shapes are slightly different, too. Asian elephants have more rounded backs. They also have trunks with one 'finger' whereas African elephants' trunks have two 'fingers'.

Asian elephants are found in India and other parts of South-east Asia.

African elephants have large ears, shaped a bit like the continent of Africa. Asian elephants' ears look a little like the outline of India.

Elephants are herbivores and a lot of their time is spent eating. The fodder they eat includes grass, shrubs, roots, fruit, leaves and branches (from up to 400 species of plant).

All African elephants have tusks, but only male Asian elephants have them. Tusks are actually big teeth and one tusk can weigh 100 kilograms. They are used for digging, lifting objects and defence.

An adult male will eat around 145 kilograms of food a day, which is the equivalent to 2,000 apples or 700 loaves of bread. Elephants only sleep for two to three hours a day and spend the rest of the time foraging.

Foraging   Sleep

Elephants can breathe while underwater by using their trunks like snorkels. They also have the strongest sense of smell of any animal on Earth.

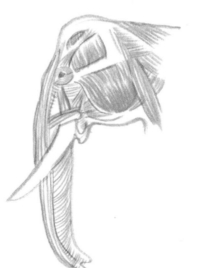

Their trunks have 40,000 muscles and can carry a 300 kilogram log or pick up a peanut. They are used for breathing, smelling, communicating and scooping up to 190 litres of water a day.

Ultrasound
(over 20,000 hertz)

Infrasound
(below 20 hertz)

Elephants have sensitive feet. They can detect low frequency sounds through vibrations in the ground. Elephants can even hear other elephants trumpeting or rumbling up to 8 kilometres away.

Elephants have big brains, protected by tough skulls, which are up to 15 centimetres thick! They are highly intelligent and emotionally sensitive, and might even mourn the death of family members.

BEHAVIOUR & HISTORY

A female is called a cow and a baby is called a calf.
A male elephant with tusks is called a bull or a tusker.

A female elephant is pregnant for 22 months.
An elephant calf will stay by its mother's side
and drink her milk for around five years.

Young elephants love to play, but young
males also fight to see who is the strongest,
occasionally breaking tusks.

Wild elephants live in groups, called herds,
of around 30 to 50 individuals and roam
great distances in search of fodder to eat.

The herd leader is usually an older female.
She and her daughters stick together,
while adult males live alone.

Tigers are the only natural predator of
Asian elephants. They tend to only attack
calves or smaller, weaker elephants.

Elephants love bathing in water and especially
enjoy mud baths, which they take to keep cool.
They are also very good swimmers.

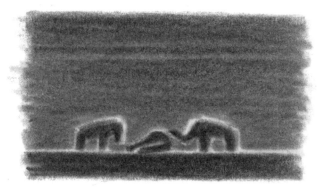

Elephants are intelligent, sensitive animals.
They have long memories and deep feelings,
with the capacity to care for friends and family.

Elephants were used for farming work
in India as early as 4,000 years ago.

Hindus believe that elephants are special
as they represent the earthly reincarnation
of the elephant-headed god, Ganesha.

During the 1600s, the Mughal Emperor Jahangir
had 113,000 elephants under his command.

Elephants are an important part of some festivals,
including the famous Jaipur Elephant Festival in India.

In some countries, elephants are used to giving
rides to tourists. Many people think this is cruel.
The animals are often treated badly and beaten.

Humans are an elephant's worst enemy. Even though
it is illegal, poachers hunt them for their beautiful
tusks, made from a hard, white material called ivory.

One hundred years ago there were around
ten million African and Asian elephants.
Sadly, today there are as few as 500,000.

For over one thousand years, elephants have
worked in the logging industry alongside humans.

A DEMANDING JOB

Between the 1920s to 1940s, around 6,000 elephants were working in the Myanmar logging industry. Though these elephants lived about twice as long as zoo elephants, their lives were tough.

Cutting down trees and shifting the gigantic logs to rivers was dangerous work. Human workers felled trees 30 metres tall and nearly 3 metres wide with just small saws and axes. The sound of the trees crashing to the ground echoed across the forest. The trunks were trimmed into shorter lengths ready to be moved by the elephants. A single tusker could haul 2-metre-wide logs weighing up to 4 tonnes, but larger logs needed two or three elephants. Williams understood the work which the timber workers, oozies and elephants did was far from easy.

Elephants were given jobs according to their strength and character. Those with a slightly curved back, like a hill, were considered best for dragging loads. Tuskers like Bandoola lifted and moved heavy logs, while smaller elephants were used for transport duties.

ELEPHANT RIDERS

Oozies are elephant riders, trainers and keepers. They take care of an elephant for its entire working life and form a close bond. An oozie's skills is passed down through the family from generation to generation.

At six year's old a child can begin training to become an oozie. At first they learn to be a pajaik, which is the name for an oozie's assistant. When they are 14 years old they are promoted to become an oozie and are responsible for their own elephant.

Elephants work about six hours a day. Annually, the elephants haul around 500,000 kilograms of timber from stump to creek. In the evenings they roam the surrounding forest foraging for food and socialising with other elephants.

A logging elephant understands up to 35 separate commands.

At dawn, oozies track down their elephant and bring them to camp to start work by 6am. They know everything about their elephant, recognising its footprint amongst hundreds of others. At the end of a day's work, the oozie will bathe their elephant and clean the entire animal from trunk to tail. A ritual that the elephants love.

An oozie can tell the exact note of the bell worn by their elephant, called a kalouk, from miles away.

 Lah! - come on!

 Phee - turn left/right

 Digo Lah! - come here!

 Hmit! - sit down!

 Yoo! - pull!

 Tah! - stand up!

 Mmah! - lift up!

 Yu/Kaut - take

 A Mot - raise your trunk

 Yoh - keep your head down

 Hong! - stop!

 A Myout - raise a foreleg

TRANSPORT

The BBTC removed 5,000,000 tonnes of timber each year during the 1920s to 1940s. Britain profited from this deforestation and, at the time, 70% of the world's teak originated from the forests of Myanmar. Using elephants meant humans could harvest timber in areas that trucks couldn't reach. Elephants are nimble and strong, whereas machinery gets stuck in mud and dense vegetation.

1

Trees are chopped down when they are 25 years or older. First, a ring is cut around the base, then the tree is left for three years to die and dry out before it is felled. The trunk is cut into logs, ready for transporting.

2

The logs are dragged along paths that are kept clear by oozies and pajaiks. Elephants pull them with chains, or use their foreheads to push them along.

3

When the rainy monsoon season arrives, the water rises and carries the logs downstream to larger rivers. Here, rafts of 125 logs are assembled and sent further downstream, to where the river widens. There, they are loaded onto barges. Occasionally elephants are used to clear log jams in the river.

4

When the logs reach the sawmills at ports like Yangon and Moulmein they are cut and seasoned, ready for exporting to other countries around the world.

Logs can travel 2,000 kilometres from stump to sawmill.
It can take up to 20 years for a log to become a milled plank.

CAPTURE AND TRAINING

Elephants had to be trained to work with humans. Williams soon learnt this was achieved through a harsh process called kheddaring. Wild elephants were captured between the ages of 15 and 20, and trapped in an enclosure called a keddah. Here they were beaten and denied food to break their spirit and force them to obey humans. It was a brutal process.

Seeing the terrible training scars on the elephants he worked with, Williams believed there had to be another way. Fortunately, Williams' friend Po Toke, a skilled oozie, had just the elephant to prove that there was…

THE PRIDE OF THE JUNGLE

At the age of 15, an oozie named Po Toke knew more about elephants than his elders.

Penniless, he believed his destiny was bound with the unborn calf of his pregnant elephant Ma Shwe.

On the night of giving birth, a tiger attacked Ma Shwe and her calf, almost killing them both.

Saved at the last minute by another member of the herd, the wounded
mother stood with her little calf trembling beneath her legs.

Po Toke was overjoyed that the baby had survived. The little calf was named 'Bandoola' after a defiant
Myanmar war general, Maha Bandula, who had fought and died for the independence of his country.

The patient Po Toke raised the podgy calf himself, training him with kindness and patience. Bandoola grew into a huge and beautiful tusker with remarkable abilities.

When Po Toke first introduced Williams to Bandoola, Williams felt an instant connection. It was said that Bandoola could do things that no other elephant could; understand many human words, identify all the tools in camp, and that he even possessed a sense of humour. Everyone wanted to be associated with him and he soon became known as the Pride of the Jungle.

ELEPHANT SCHOOL

Po Toke had shown Williams that it was possible to train a calf without violence, and that the result was much better than with a wild kheddared elephant. Bandoola was strong, gentle and worked well with humans. Williams wanted to set up a school so other elephants could be trained in this way too. After months of persuading his bosses, Williams was finally granted permission.

Po Toke and Williams worked together to create a place where elephants could be trained compassionately.

While Williams used his position of power to make changes and oversee the running of the school, Po Toke became the head teacher.

Younger elephants watched and learnt from koonkies (older, well-tempered elephants), while oozies could share their knowledge with each other. It was better for the elephants and better for business, too. Here strong bonds could be built and the complexity of an elephant's emotions could be nurtured. Williams respected the Buddhist belief system that had fostered such a loving relationship between humans and elephants in Myanmar.

ELEPHANT HOSPITAL

After the success of the elephant school, Williams decided to start an elephant hospital. Elephants came into the hospital for all kinds of reasons, including wounds from tiger attacks, fluid-filled lumps called cysts and other infections, all of which Williams tended to. He had no formal medical training but he was able to learn how to help the elephants from the oozies. Once, he even nursed Bandoola back to health for a whole year after a fight with a wild tusker.

As he cared for them, Williams saw how kindness and patience helped the elephants to trust him. He supposed it was the same for people too.

From his experiences at the elephant school and hospital, Williams learnt so much. He had already admired elephants for their size, strength and intelligence, but now he came to feel that they were the most magnificent of all animals.

Bandoola became the star pupil of Po Toke and Williams' new approach to working with elephants. Being born in the same year, Williams always felt that he and Bandoola were kindred spirits. As time passed, Bandoola became stronger and stronger, as did his bond with humans.

BANDOOLA TO THE RESCUE

In 1927, Williams himself needed medical help. He had fallen ill with a disease called malaria. Too weak to move, he felt as though each day was a step closer to death. It was a ten-day trek to find help; the only route was through miles of forest to reach aid on the banks of the Chindwin River. It was Bandoola's turn to provide care to Williams. Putting all trust in his friend, Williams clambered on to Bandoola's back and was carried sick and unconscious through the jungle, eventually finding help days later.

A NEW DANGER

After recovering from malaria, Williams continued overseeing the timber transportation, training calves at the elephant school and caring for sick animals at the elephant hospital. But in 1942, a darkness came over the jungle. World War II had broken out in 1939 between the Axis powers (Germany, Italy and Japan) and the Allies (Great Britain, France, and later the USA, China and Russia).

Even in the remote rainforest, war had found Williams again. It threatened his life and those he had befriended over the last 22 years. The world war had grown so vast that it was now raging between the British and the Japanese, leaving the Myanmar people caught in between. As the Japanese army invaded Myanmar, elephants, oozies and all camp inhabitants were now in mortal danger. Life as Williams and Bandoola had known it was about to change forever.

ANOTHER WAR

With World War II upon them, Williams desperately wanted to help the Allied side. He joined 'Force 136', a branch of the British secret service, based in the deep jungles of South-east Asia and put together a special team of expert oozies and 46 elephants.

  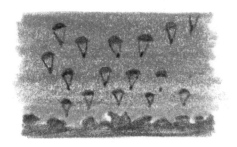

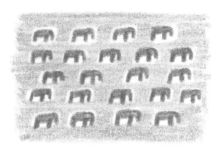

It was as if the elephant school had been preparing for this moment, without even knowing it. Now it was time to show the world what these amazing animals could do.

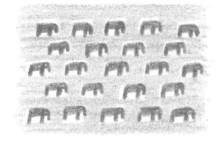

The team was known as 'Elephant Company' and led by Bandoola, 'Number One War Elephant'. They would help the British by building hundreds of bridges, widening paths, and carrying supplies and weapons.

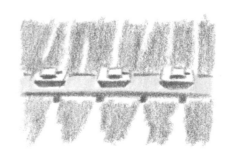

One of Williams' main objectives was rescuing elephants from behind enemy lines. Gradually he built up his company. At the peak of the campaign, Williams had 1,600 elephants and their oozies helping the war effort.

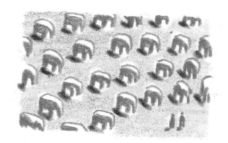

THE GREAT ELEPHANT RESCUE

Elephant Company's operations were going well until March 1944, when Williams received sudden orders to evacuate the jungle and travel to the safety of Assam, India, which was in British territory. The Japanese army were closing in, while the British and their allies were planning a counter attack. His heart sank. He knew he would have to abandon everything he had worked on so hard.

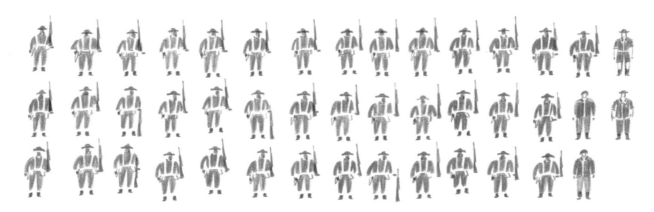

He couldn't bear to leave his friends at the camp behind, as he knew the fate of those that stayed would not be a kind one. So he decided to take them with him. Williams, Po Toke and his Elephant Company would escort refugees, oozies and elephants out of the conflict. The party consisted of 64 women and children, 53 elephants, 40 armed soldiers, 90 oozies and assistants and four British military officers. What would follow would be one of the most miraculous escape missions the world had ever seen.

HIMALAYAS

IMPHAL

WANJING

TAMU

CHINDWIN RIVER

MYANMAR

People thought Williams' plan was foolish. The Chief Field Doctor declined to join Williams, saying: "I'd rather stay here and starve, Bill!" But Williams kept his chin up and ignored the others' negativity.

Leaving Myanmar would be treacherous and Williams knew they had to be prepared for anything. Stretching out before them was 190 kilometres of perilous jungle, with countless towering mountains, as well as the very real threat of attacks from tigers or human enemies.

INTO THE UNKNOWN

Despite the dangers, the party started their journey. The threat of ambush hung over them like a dark shadow, but Williams was lifted by the cheerfulness of the oozies and the refugees' strength of spirit. The dense jungle seemed to sprawl forever as they trekked deeper into its depths.

A SEA OF JUNGLE

They soon reached the mountains and began to climb. The party ascended over 1,500 metres and although progress was torturous for the refugees, they never complained. Occasionally, they were rewarded with beautiful panoramic views of the lush, misty mountain range extending into the distance.

DIFFICULT TERRAIN

For all the beauty of the jungle, it could not make up for the difficult, and at times impassable, terrains the group faced. As time went on, the condition of the party was deteriorating. Williams kept the weakest at the front and the strongest carried as much of the burden as possible.

Day by day people became thinner, hungrier and weaker. They began to suffer from sores, malaria, altitude sickness, fever, dysentery, pneumonia and abscesses.

As trails disappeared, the vegetation grew thicker and all consuming. Progress was slow, as men and women had to hack away at the undergrowth with machetes.

Not only were people falling ill, but the elephants were too. While older elephants collapsed under the strain, Bandoola, the Pride of the Jungle thrived, crashing his way through the trees.

At nightfall, cool rain fell, while the enemy guns rang out in the darkness.
The unit huddled together and prayed for morning.

On some days the terrain would become easier and they felt some relief,
though the fear of enemy ambush always remained.

THE ELEPHANT STAIRWAY

After nine gruelling days, the group found themselves at an impasse: an enormous wall of rock towered above them. Feeling defeated, they rested for two days while Williams and Po Toke hatched an impossible plan. There was no other choice, they would climb over it by building an elephant stairway into the rockface.

For days the oozies cut steps into the sandstone that connected the flatter ledges. It would be the ultimate test of courage and trust; if one elephant were to fall or panic it could be catastrophic for all involved. Looking on, Williams confessed his fear to Po Toke. With a gentle smile, Po Toke told him not to worry: Bandoola would be leading them.

Finally, the stairway was complete. It was time to go. Po Toke called, "Thwar!" and Bandoola started to climb. One by one, the elephants followed. Williams, who suffered from vertigo, crawled behind them. "If we could not do it now, we never would. One thing we knew was there was no turning back," Williams said.

AN IMPOSSIBLE CLIMB

Higher and higher they climbed, while gunfire rang out in the distance. The enemy was near. Silently and precisely, Bandoola moved up the stairway, sometimes pausing tentatively while everyone held their breath.

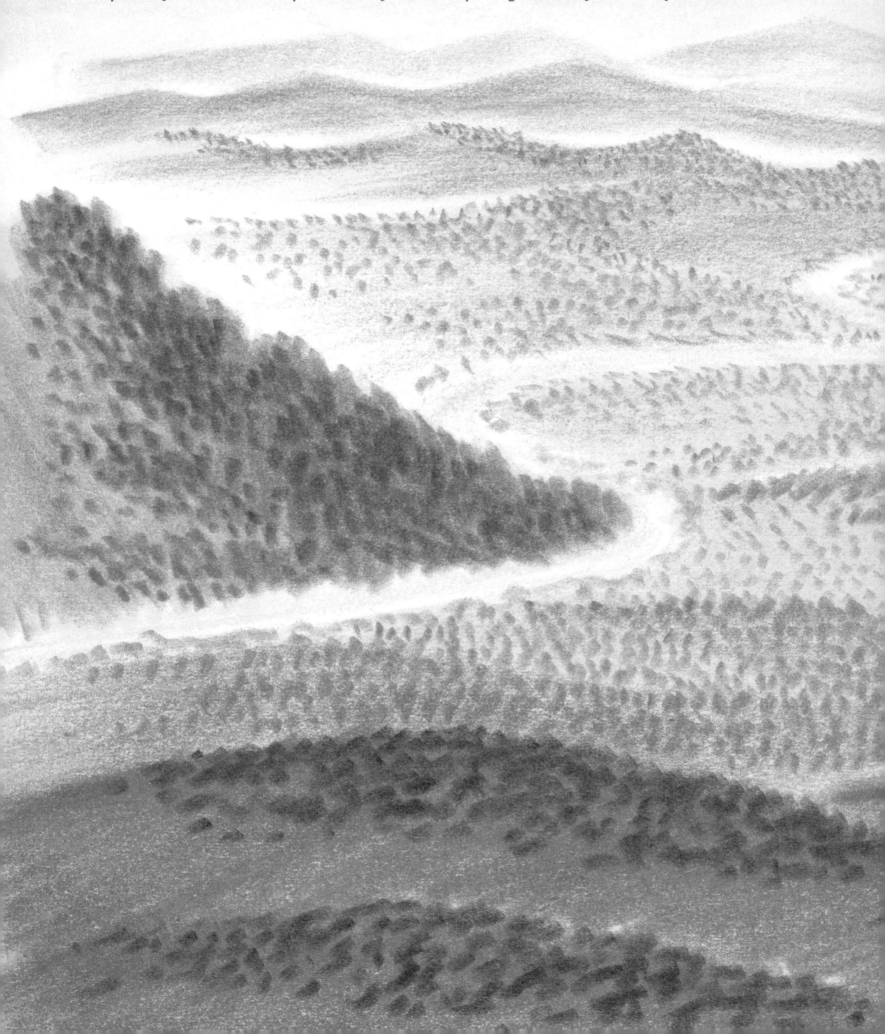

REACHING THE TOP

Finally, the stairway came to an end. For three hours from base to summit, Bandoola had done what was asked of him. His legs shook upon reaching the top, but his endurance and spirit had held firm. "I learned more in that one day about what elephants could be got to do than I had in 24 years . . . it was a moment of greatness, a heroic moment in which Po Toke had his full share," Williams said. He had put his trust in Bandoola, and his friend had come through for him. Their bond was the strongest it had ever been.

END IN SIGHT

The next day, they crossed into British territory and an immense weight was lifted. Despite being safe from enemy capture, there were still eight days of gruelling journey left. Impenetrable bamboo forest, quicksand and the burden of illness in the party were all significant threats.

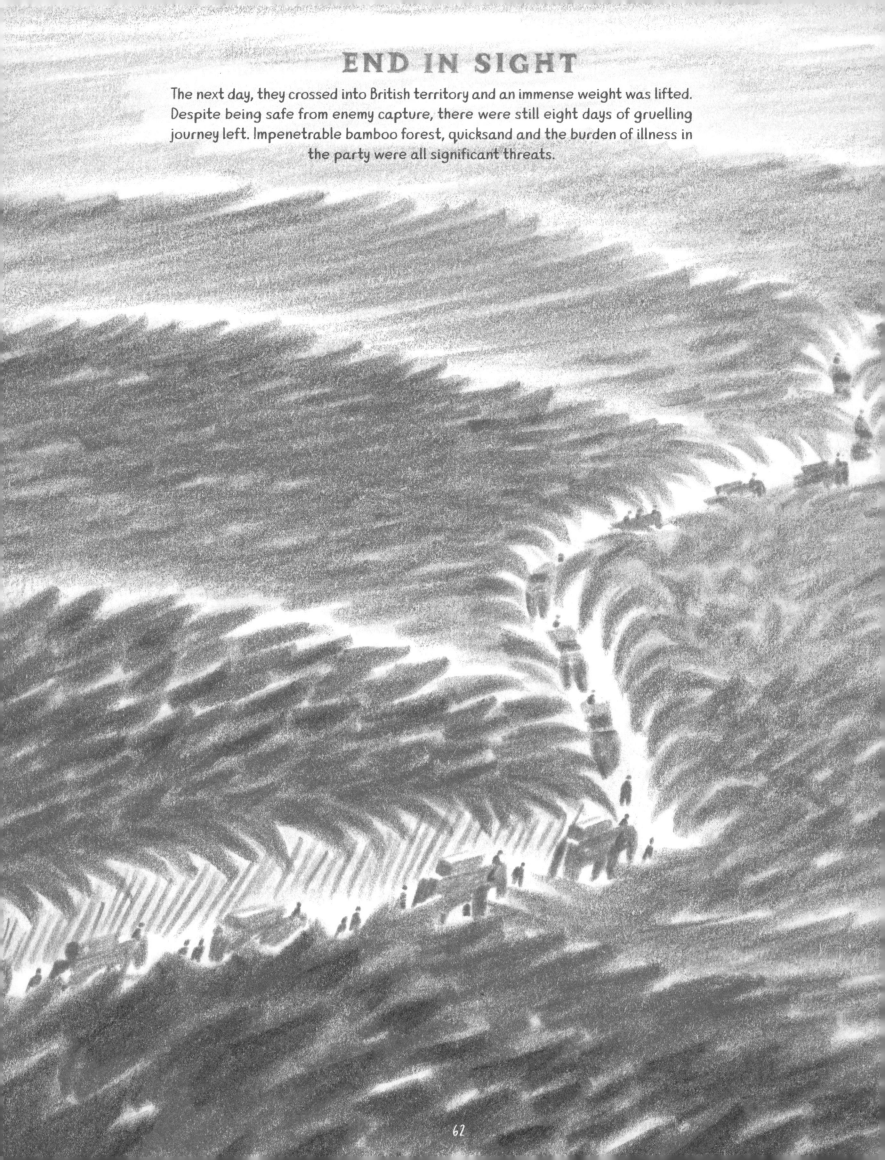

With rations running low they were each provided with a small matchbox portion of rice per day. The unit had to eat whatever the jungle provided to survive. The elephants, however, enjoyed the bounty of fodder the jungle had to offer. Having scaled the wall of rock, hope was rekindled, and it continued to grow as they inched closer to safety.

SAFE AT LAST

On 26th April 1944, three weeks after leaving the camp, they arrived at their destination, a tea plantation in Assam. The great journey was over. Children were taken away for immediate care while some people were reunited with their families. They had further reason to celebrate when they learnt that the Japanese were retreating in Myanmar. Elephant Company would rest at the refuge for four months.

DREAMING OF FREEDOM

Williams was sad that his life with elephants was drawing to an end. His life in Myanmar could never be the same, his Burmese and British friends had now fled too. As the light faded on a good day, Bandoola lowered his head to look Williams in the eye. They stood together quietly, savouring the moment of peace between them.

After all the hard work and heroic deeds that the elephants had performed to help humans, Williams and Po Toke dreamt they would now find freedom. Although he had worked hard to improve their working conditions, he found himself wanting more for them. He imagined some of those brave elephants still in Myanmar would be lost to war, but many would have escaped into the jungle and found their wild relatives, just like they had done in their logging days. Williams wrote: "Herds of wild elephants show no resentment when domesticated animals join them. This tolerance is just one of the things about elephants which makes one realise they are big in more ways than one."

THE STRUGGLE CONTINUES

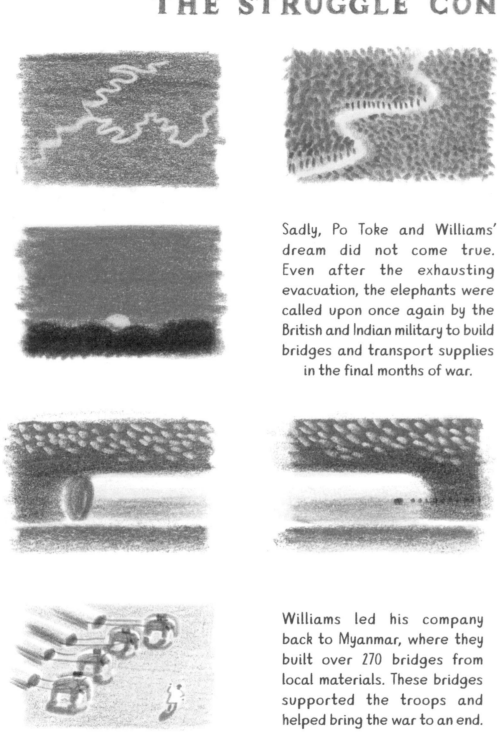

Sadly, Po Toke and Williams' dream did not come true. Even after the exhausting evacuation, the elephants were called upon once again by the British and Indian military to build bridges and transport supplies in the final months of war.

Williams led his company back to Myanmar, where they built over 270 bridges from local materials. These bridges supported the troops and helped bring the war to an end.

Bridges also enabled civilians to flee conflict areas and precious supplies and vehicles to be transported through inaccessible terrain.

In December 1944, Elephant Company built the largest known Bailey bridge across the Chindwin River. Their work would help change the course of history.

A SAD FAREWELL

Williams became a decorated war hero and the press appropriately named him "Elephant Bill". He knew none of it would've been possible without his good friends Po Toke and Bandoola who both deserved respect and recognition, too. Before leaving Myanmar, Williams went on a long journey to say farewell to the 417 elephants he could find. Bandoola was missing.

FALLEN FRIEND

Williams didn't want to leave without saying goodbye and was hopeful his friend would appear. A search party scanned the surrounding area and Bandoola was eventually found. The great tusker lay motionless on the ground, with a tusk sawn off. It looked like the work of a poacher. Bandoola had been betrayed by the same creatures he had trusted for so many years.

Williams searched to find the culprit without success. Heartbroken, he left
a mark by Bandoola's grave: "Bandoola: Born 1897, killed in action 1944."

BANDOOLA'S LEGACY

After all that the elephants had done to help humans, Williams believed they deserved to be treated with kindness and respect more than ever. For him, the connection between an oozie and an elephant proved that humans could live peacefully side by side with the animal kingdom. It was a choice that could be made.

Looking back on his time in Myanmar Williams reflected that: "I have found my happiness not in considering myself a *Homo sapien* set apart from the rest of creation, but in seeing that I fit in with the rest of nature, what are called so wrongly the animal and vegetable kingdoms. I believe that plants and animals have an immediate sensitiveness, an awareness of loving, of what is good and what is perilous, that we humans cut ourselves off from to our own detriment, that is what the jungle has taught me."

EPILOGUE

Though this story is set over 75 years ago, there is still much we can learn from Bandoola's tale.

Williams and Po Toke's work has influenced the care and training of elephants to the present day. Today, thousands of elephants continue to work alongside oozies in Myanmar, most are well cared for and work less than they used to. Myanmar has more elephant experts than any other Asian country and the country is a world leader in elephant care and oozie skills. In 2018, The Myanmar Elephant Conservation Action Plan was launched to protect wild elephants and their habitat.

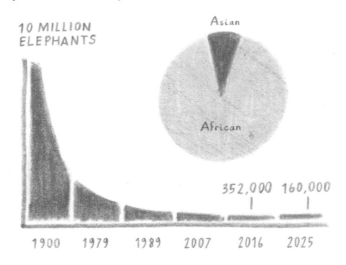

10 MILLION ELEPHANTS

Asian

African

352,000   160,000

1900   1979   1989   2007   2016   2025

Despite this, some elephants are not so fortunate as kheddaring is still practised illegally in parts of Asia. Perhaps more concerning is the threat from poachers, who hunt and kill elephants for their ivory.

Across the world, elephant populations are declining rapidly, and humans are largely to blame. As well as the threat from poaching, we have destroyed large areas of their habitats.

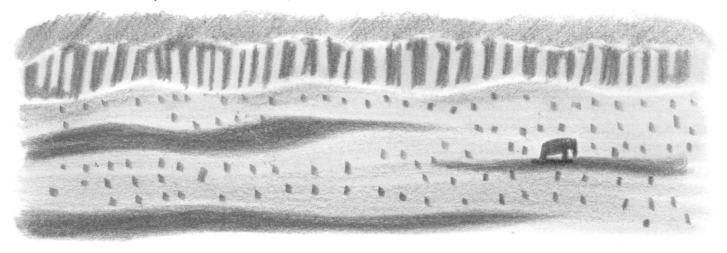

In the early 1900s, it was estimated that Asia was home to over 100,000 elephants. In 2021, that number was as low as 40,000. That is one tenth of the population of African elephants. The future of elephants hangs in the balance; will we protect them and their habitat, or continue along the path we are on? Ultimately it is up to us.

Even though we know elephants are intelligent and sensitive, we've used them to meet our own needs for thousands of years. Elephants have served humans as living tanks in wars, as status symbols, as tractors and transporters, as amusements at the circus or zoo, and as ornaments on our walls. Perhaps the final stage in our relationship with these animals will be a different one, one where we respect their right to be free.

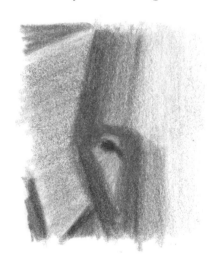

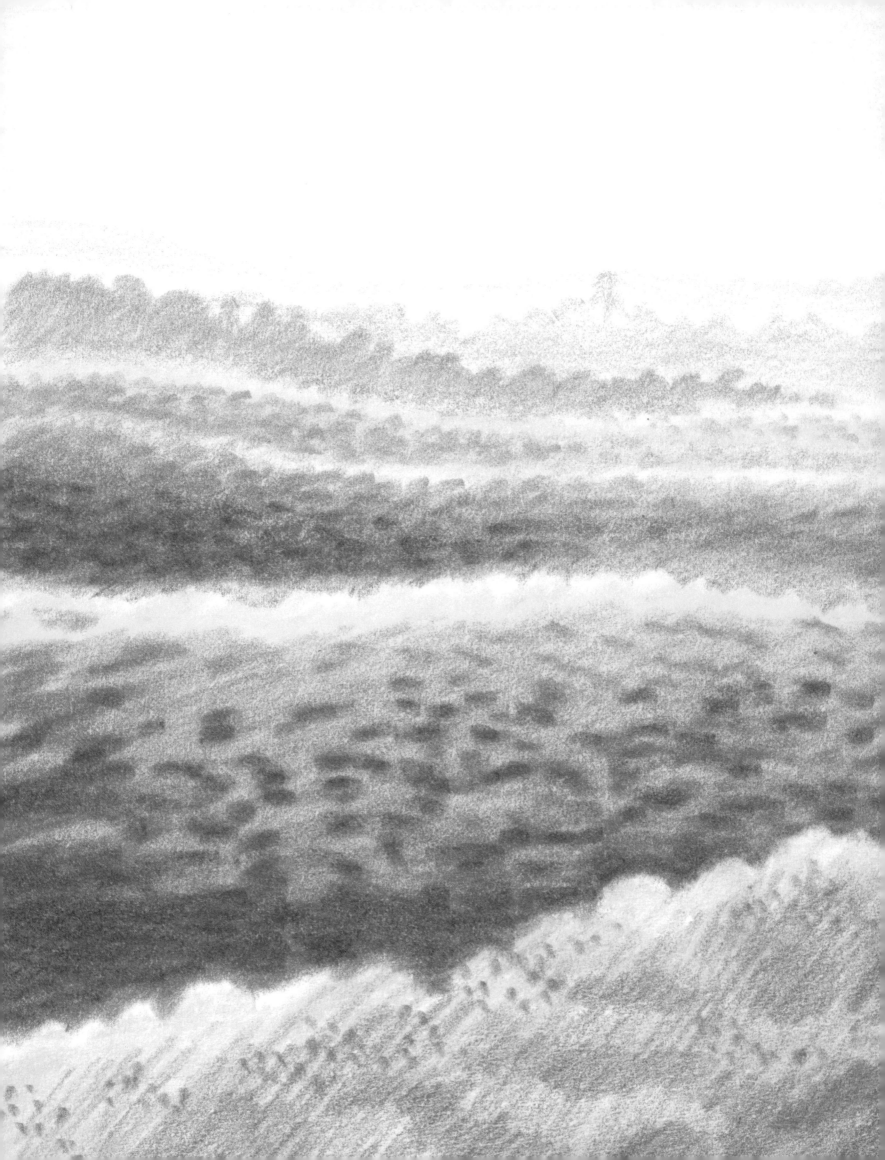

GLOSSARY

Altitude sickness
A life threatening sickness that occurs at high altitude

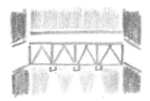

Bailey Bridge
A portable, prefabricated bridge used in World War II

Bamboo
Tall, dense, thick stick-like grass

Biome
Areas of our planet with similiar climates, animals and plants

Bull
A male elephant

Calf
A baby elephant

Cow
A female elephant

Deforestation
When forests are cut down by humans

Dysentery
An infection of the intestines

Force 136
A branch of the British World War II secret service, based in the jungles of South-east Asia

Fodder
Elephant food

General Maha Bandula
A Myanmar general who fought against the British in the First Anglo-Burmese War

Herd
A group of elephants

Ivory
A hard white material from the tusks of animals including elephants

Kalouk
Teak bell around an elephant's neck

Karen people
Ethnic group native to
Kayin state, Myanmar

Kheddaring
The practice of capturing and
training mature wild elephants

Malaria
A disease carried by mosquitoes

Mughal
The Mughal Empire ruled most of
northern India from the 1500s to the 1700s

Oozie
An elephant rider, trainer
and keeper

Pagoda
A Buddhist temple

Pajaik
A ground assistant to an oozie

Proboscidea
The group of animals
which elephants belong to

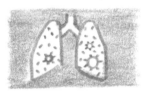

Pneumonia
Lung inflammation caused
by bacteria or a virus

Quicksand
Waterlogged sand, which sucks in
anything resting on or falling into it

Reincarnation
A person or animal in which another
soul, sometimes of a god, is reborn

Teak
Precious hardwood
harvested for exporting

Timber
Wood that is used to
build houses and buildings

Tusker
A male elephant with tusks

Vertigo
A sickness and dizziness that paralyses
some people at heights

APPENDIX & FURTHER READING

Books

Elephant Bill, James Howard Williams, Penguin, 1956

Bandoola, James Howard Williams, Rupert Hart-Davis, 1953

Elephant Company, Vicki Croke, Random House Trade, 2015

Giants of The Monsoon Forest: Living And Working with Elephants, Jacob Shell, W. W. Norton & Company, 2019

The Burma Campaign, Frank McLynn, Vintage, 2011

Chindit 1942-45, Tim Moreman, Osprey Publishing, 2009

Locations

Greenhill Valley Elephant Sanctuary, Kalaw, Myanmar: https://ghvelephant.com

MTE Elephant Camp, Bago Jungle, Myanmar

Websites

https://elephant-project.science/timber-elephants/

https://www.nationalgeographic.com/animals/mammals/facts/asian-elephant

https://www.worldwildlife.org/species/asian-elephant

http://www.fao.org/3/ad031e/ad031e0d.htm

http://www.bbc.co.uk/history/worldwars/wwtwo/burma_campaign_01.shtml

https://globalelephants.org/in-depth-facts/

AUTHOR'S NOTE

Many years ago I came across the book 'Elephant Bill' in a second hand bookshop in Falmouth. The story of Bandoola resonated with me not just because of its incredible visual potential, but because it had an important message too. There are many great values we can learn from our connections with animals such as patience, loyalty and trust. Bandoola's story made me realise that elephants are not only big and beautiful, but they can be courageous and trusting too.

In February 2020, I visited Myanmar as part of my research for this book. While there I met and observed working oozies and their elephants in the jungle. I also spent some time at Greenhill Valley Elephant Camp, an ethical sanctuary which cares for retired timber elephants. Their aim is to educate and share information with local and foreign visitors. The trip not only allowed me to make observational drawings of elephants and their environment, but learn from the people who know them best and appreciate these extraordinary animals in person.

The subject of timber elephants is a complex one. As tough as their working life can be, currently there are some benefits that come from our interactions with them. As an endangered species, Asian timber elephants are kept safe from poachers and they do not interfere with rural human settlements and farmland. The oozie population of Myanmar is the largest in the world and this represents a huge knowledge base in further understanding the health and wellbeing of elephants in a rapidly changing world. The selective logging system with elephants is more sustainable than other logging methods and has meant that the forests have been less intruded upon than if a more mechanised approach had been used.

Still, we all hope for a future where elephants can live peacefully together, with and without human contact and where they're free to roam in their natural habitat.

If you enjoyed Bandoola: The Great Elephant Rescue,
read William Grill's award-winning books
Shackleton's Journey and *The Wolves of Currumpaw*

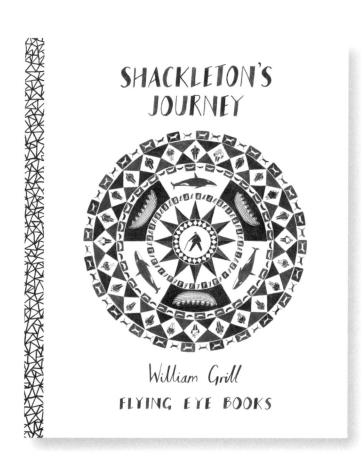

9781909263109

'A book every house should have.'
-The Guardian

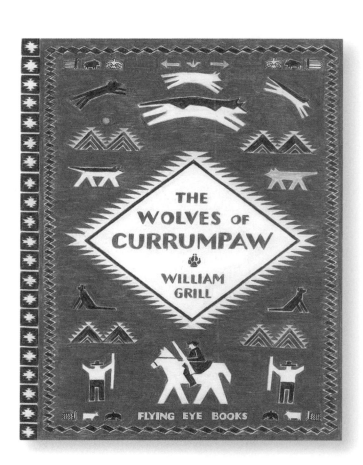

9781909263833

'Grill has created a powerful picture book
that is certain to provoke feelings of
empathy for the regal Lobo and Blanca.'

-New York Times

First edition published in 2021 by Flying Eye Books,
an imprint of Nobrow Ltd. 27 Westgate Street, London, E8 3RL.

Text and illustrations © William Grill 2021.
Consultant: Jennie Crawley

Every attempt has been made to ensure any statements written as fact have been checked
to the best of our abilities. However, we are still human, thankfully, and occasionally
little mistakes may crop up. Should you spot any errors, please email info@nobrow.net.

1 3 5 7 9 10 8 6 4 2

Published in the US by Nobrow (US) Inc.

Printed in Poland

ISBN: 978-1-83874-023-8

www.flyingeyebooks.com

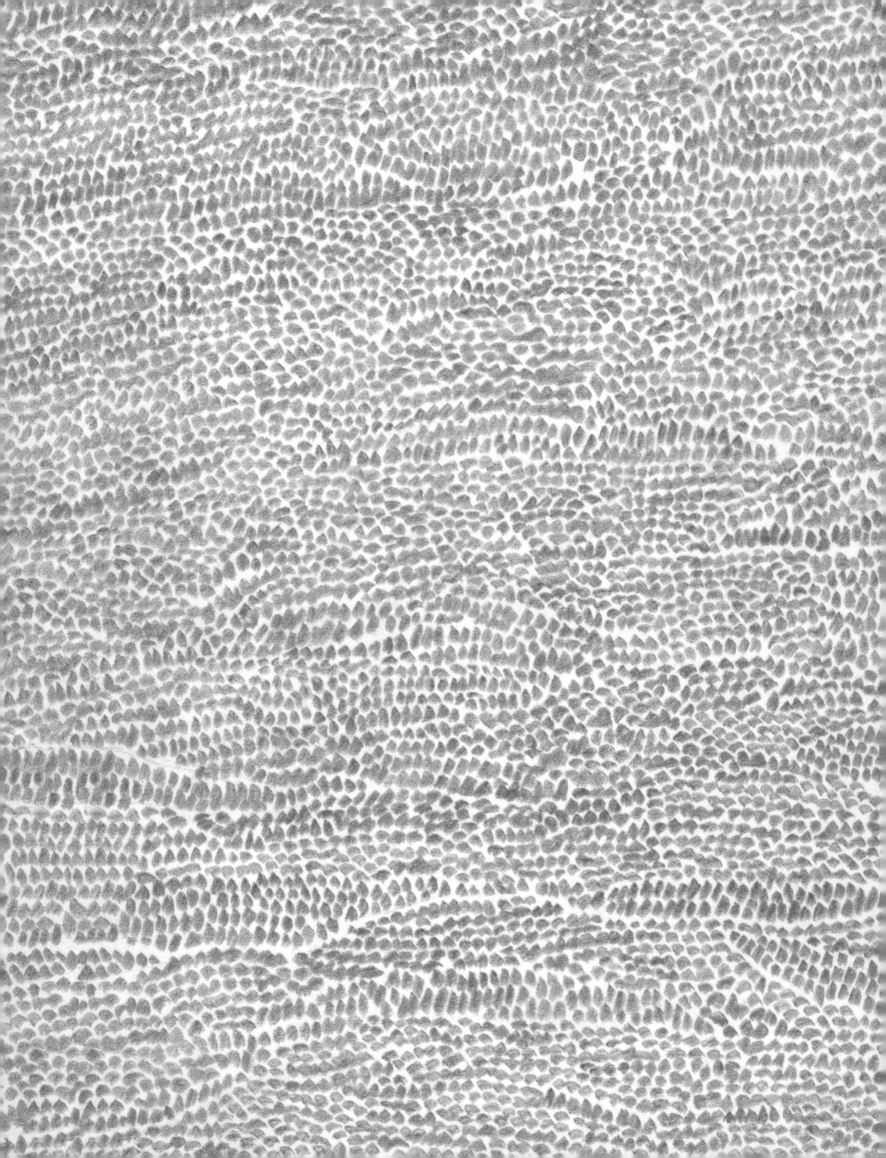